Steam Memories: 1950's – 1960's

No. 47: SOUTH WEST SCOTLA

Pictures by **Neville Stead**

Copyright Book Law Publications 2012
ISBN 978-1-907094-26-2

INTRODUCTION

We are about to embark on an imaginary journey around south-west Scotland starting, appropriately, at Glasgow's St Enoch station. We will be visiting real places as they existed in the post-war days of the 50s and the following 'decade of change' – the 60s. We are going to take a look at what it was like in those not too far-off days when most of the infrastructure, services and staff were still plentiful and a railway journey was an experience of sorts and was the only way to travel any distance in relative comfort and safety. Hopefully the illustrations herein will bring back nostalgic memories of what it was once like on the railway system of south-west Scotland.

Neville Stead has supplied the bulk of the illustrations contained herein and the Publisher would like to thank him for sorting through his vast collection to find these particular gems. Two other people, namely Ian Trivett and Neill Fisher, have supplied much of the information regarding the rolling stock featured in this album and we would like to thank them both for sharing their knowledge with us.

Cover Picture (see Page 26)

(previous page) **With a local passenger working from Harbour station to Kilmarnock on Monday 22nd May 1961, 2P No.40661 exits the southern point of the triangle (Holm junction) where Ardrossan engine shed was built in 1894. The line obscured by the 4-4-0's exhaust, and veering to the right of the engine shed (also partly obscured), was the direct route to Largs. That direct route necessitated the building of the next station where the train will call on its journey east – Ardrossan (South Beach). No.40661 was a Hurlford based 2P and near to withdrawal.**

Printed and bound by The Amadeus Press, Cleckheaton, West Yorkshire
First published in the United Kingdom by Book Law Publications, 382 Carlton Hill, Nottingham, NG4 1JA

It seems appropriate to start a journey to south-west Scotland from the Glasgow terminus of the erstwhile Glasgow & South Western Railway – St Enoch. It is Monday 19th April 1965 and according to the station clock it is a little before 10.30 a.m.. Standing at platform 4 is a Corkerhill based BR Standard Class 4, No.76093, at the head of a stopping service to the west, probably Ardrossan, Largs, Ayr or Kilmarnock. The departure is one of the supposedly 250 trains, carrying 23,000 passengers, which used the terminus each day by this time, and which would be diverted to nearby Central station in just over a year, when this one-time edifice to the might of the railways was closed. Opened fully in 1879, St Enoch became the headquarters of the Glasgow & South Western Railway and was their showpiece station complete with its own 200-room hotel and direct services to London via the Midland Railway, not to mention direct services to west coast sea ports for sailings to Ireland and even destinations in England. The 204 foot wide span of the great arch we are looking at covered six platforms and until westward extensions to the station were carried out in 1902, handled a thriving passenger clientele successfully. The height of the span was measured as 83 ft above the rail and the whole shed was 525 ft long – impressive indeed. The similarity between this arched roof and that of London's St Pancras station, not to mention Manchester (Central) too, is easy to understand considering the Midland influence at this station and the Manchester terminus. Not only that, the company which supplied the metalwork and erected those same arches was one and the same – A.Handyside of Derby. So, having covered some of St Enoch's history let the journey begin. Be warned, there is no particular geographical order to the presentation of the illustrations.

3

Caley 3P No.54468 makes a spirited departure from Greenock (Princes Pier) with the five-coach 1.30 p.m. Saturdays Only to Glasgow (St Enoch) on 22nd June 1957. The forthcoming 1 in 70 gradient and the tunnel did not make life easy for engine crews working out of Princes Pier. A rail service from Princes Pier to Glasgow was offered by the G&SWR from 1869 onwards but from 1889 the Caledonian Railway spoilt the South Western's virtual monopoly when it opened the line from Gourock and offered the residents and commuters of Greenock, not to mention the folk who used the Clyde steamers, a shorter journey time to Glasgow. From then on the commuter services from Princes Pier declined to the point that, by 1966 when the station and line closed, only boat trains offered any traffic. Resident at Greenock shed since just before World War II, this particular 4-4-0 had previously been allocated to the former CR shed at Perth but moved out when that establishment was rebuilt. With a little over two years service still to do, No.54468 was looking rather tired but still obviously able to perform. Just peeking into the frame is the wall of Princes Pier engine shed and in the yard beyond a number of locomotives are laid up for the weekend or otherwise; identifiable are one of the Greenock based 3F 0-6-0s No.57682, and recently withdrawn 4-4-0 No.54441.

A little later during that Saturday in June 1957, a service from Glasgow runs down towards Princes Pier with a clean Cl.4 tank in charge, Ladyburn's own No.42247. As mentioned, the commuter services to and from Princes Pier were somewhat scant by the Fifties but the station had its 'moments' of intense activity during the decade: Writing in the *Railway Magazine* in 1952 W.A.C.Smith mentioned that apart from a few Atlantic liner specials, traffic at the station had not been heavy since the end of WW2 because the Clyde steamers no longer used the pier. However, during three days in September some 75 warships visited the Clyde in readiness for the forthcoming NATO exercise 'Mainbrace'. Five special Leave trains were run each day on Wednesday 10th, Thursday 11th and Friday 12th, from Princes Pier station to Paisley and Glasgow (St Enoch). The trains departed from Greenock between 2.15 p.m. and 3.20 p.m. and were each made up of eight non-corridor coaches with motive power consisting 4P 2-6-4Ts from Corkerhill and also Hughes 2-6-0s from Kingmoor! The only former CR 4-4-0 at Ladyburn shed during that period was borrowed to act as station pilot. To add further activity, three public excursions from St Enoch to Princes Pier carried passengers for specially laid-on cruises around the gathered fleet – every day! A dampener was put on proceedings on the 11th when a derailment of some wagons disorganised the traffic arrangements and two of the excursions were cancelled. Not to be left out of proceedings, Gourock also handled six additional leave trains during the visit of the fleet whilst two were also run from Helensburgh on the north bank.

Corkerhill based Class 4 tank No.42123 works a ten-coach, late morning Gourock-Glasgow (St Enoch) service past Greenock Ladyburn engine shed on Saturday 16th August 1958. This is a typical summer Saturday working moving people from the city to the coast and vice versa. The normal Gourock-Wemyss Bay passenger trains to and from Glasgow worked into Central station and were handled by Class 4 tanks from Polmadie and Greenock Ladyburn. The latter depot had a number of these useful 2-6-4T allocated, mainly of the Fowler and Fairburn varieties. During the 50s' and 60s' the following came and went: 42175 and 42176 arrived new in November 1948 and worked from the shed until withdrawn. They complemented the seven Fowler side-window tanks, Nos.42417 to 42423, which in March 1954 transferred to the London Midland Region to be swapped for more Fairburn engines – 42236 from Stoke, 42258 to 42261 from Bangor, 42262 to 42265 from Monument Lane, and 42266 from Springs Branch. In January 1955 these were supplemented by 42238 to 42241 from Polmadie, followed by others from 66A as follows: 42247 December 1956, 42245 August 1961, 42060 October 1961, 42242 December 1961. Some, but not many of these engines eventually moved away from Ladyburn with 42236 returning to the LMR in February 1960 whilst 42238 and 42247 moved to Corkerhill in January 1959, with No.42239 going to Polmadie in the same period. Others which came and went include 42688 and 42690 from Polmadie in September 1954, these moving on to Beattock and Dundee Tay Bridge in January 1955; 42691 and 42698 from Polmadie in December 1952, to Dundee January 1955 and Newton Heath in February 1960 respectively. In April 1960 No.42691 returned from Tay Bridge before moving to St Margarets in January 1964. No.42692 also came from Dundee in April 1960 and stayed. 42694 arrived from Dawsholm in July 1964 but transferred to Carstairs in May 1965. Two of the more notable allocations which occurred in BR days was the arrival in September 1951 of the 3-cylinder ex LT&SR line LMS Stanier 4P tanks Nos.42530 and 42535 which were tried out with a view to their eventual ousting from the Essex route by electrification. Both returned to Plaistow in March and May 1952 respectively. Between December 1962 and July 1966 the Class 4 tanks were picked off for scrapping one by one but as one fell Polmadie supplied another; for instance 42170 August 1964; 42216 March 1964; Dawsholm sent 42197 in October 1964. These in turn were backed up by the arrival of three or four BR Standard Cl.4 tanks. Our subject locomotive No.42123 arrived new at Corkerhill in September 1949, moved on to Ardrossan in February 1960 and finally transferred to the North Eastern Region at Neville Hill shed in September 1963. Withdrawal took place five months later. This is the nearest it got to Greenock Ladyburn shed.

Class 4 No.42260 arrives at Gourock with a morning service from Glasgow on Monday 19th April 1965. On the right Polmadie's Standard Cl.4 No.80027 is ready to work back to Glasgow bunker first. The suburban train services between Glasgow (Central), Gourock and Wemyss Bay had always been intensive with maximum utilisation necessary from the dedicated batch of coaching stock. During most of the BR period some seventeen, five-coach, sets were allocated but these were often strengthened to eight or ten coaches at peak times and during seasonal requirements. In 1951 the basic sets, all non-corridor, were made up as follows: brake-third, third, first, third, brake-third, with seats for 64 first and 360 third class passengers. On a summer Saturday, again in 1951 but basically remaining unchanged throughout the decade, one such set would be worked thus:

Depart	From	To	Arrive
8.25 a.m.	Wemyss Bay	Glasgow Cen.	9.23 a.m.
9.50 a.m.	Glasgow Cen.	Gourock	10.41 a.m.
11.32 a.m.	Gourock	Glasgow Cen.	12.35 p.m.
12.55 p.m.	Glasgow Cen.	Wemyss Bay	1.53 p.m.
3.55 p.m.	Wemyss Bay	Glasgow Cen.	4.36 p.m.
5.20 p.m.	Glasgow Cen.	Gourock	6.12 p.m.
6.45 p.m.	Gourock	Glasgow Cen.	8.02 p.m.
8.30 p.m.	Glasgow Cen.	Gourock	9.18 p.m.
10.10 p.m.	Gourock	Glasgow Cen.	11.16 p.m.

The set was then stabled overnight at Glasgow (Central) station to form the 6.55 a.m. service to Gourock on Sunday morning. This intensity had of course been the norm on these two routes for decades before and would only change when electrification was introduced and multiple units would then become subject to similar use. It is something of a tribute to the Class 4 tank engines that they were able to work and keep to time with the ten-coach formations just as much as when hauling a five-coach set.

BR Standard Cl.4 2-6-4T No.80128 approaches Lugton with a St Enoch to Kilmarnock stopping service on Saturday 16th May 1959. Lugton was the junction for Beith (Town) branch line, a Joint CR/G&SWR undertaking some five miles long. The passenger service on the branch was, by May 1959, worked by a diesel railbus and one of the A.C. Cars 4-wheel vehicles, SC79976, can be seen stabled in the goods yard waiting to pick up Beith passengers from the Kilmarnock train.

Beith (Town) on that same Saturday in May 1959. The Joint terminus presented a tidy uncluttered vista with the coal yard still busy and the goods shed holding its own although it was probably out of use by now. The station building appears to be well cared for with evidence of a recent paint job having been completed. During my younger days I had a theory that every time BR got out the paint, renewed the ballast or upgraded the signalling at a location where nothing had obviously been spent for years or even decades, the said location receiving the 'make-over' was about to close. Lo and behold, within two years the deed was usually done and another station, or whole branch line was closed. Of course not all of the closed 'places' had been worked on prior to closure. That exercise only came into affect at those places where certain opposition might be forthcoming and it was deemed that the 'costs outstrip revenue' argument would have to be brought into the equation. Beith (Town) was regarded as one of those locations. Opened in June 1873, the branch had latterly been worked by ex CR 0-4-4Ts with the occasional ex LMS 2P 4-4-0 or 0-6-0, both LMS and ex CR, turning up from Hurlford. Passenger services on the branch in 1958 saw the arrival of four-wheel railbuses with the AC type (*see* previous illustration) vehicles sharing the traffic with a Bristol/ Eastern Coach Works railbus, SC79958.

The view to the south and east from Beith (Town) platform on 16th May 1959. The line disappears off to Lugton, via Barrmill, beneath the bridge seen above the permanent way hut on the left of the yard. Note the disused engine shed at the top of the yard. Opened with the branch, the shed had closed with the introduction of the railbus services. Beith (Town) station eventually closed to passengers on Bonfire Night 1962. On the main line a little to the west of this terminus, the G&SW had their own passenger station, Beith (North), which had opened in 1840 but had been closed by BR in June 1951.

Moving on to the coast now, we come across locally based Caley 3F No.57590 working a short empty mineral train from the harbour branch through Ardrossan (Town) station in 1957. Ardrossan was well catered for when it came to passenger stations. Town station dated from circa 1840 and along with what became known as Harbour station, was opened by the G&SWR. South Beach station was another such establishment opened by the G&SWR and that was built in 1883 on the direct route to Largs, which enabled St Enoch to Largs services to connect with Ardrossan without the need to work into Town station and then reverse direction, requiring another engine.

The erstwhile Ardrossan (North) station in 1957. Besides those supplied by the G&SWR, which incidentally chose the prime sites it seems, and are still open for business, the Caledonian Railway built their own station on the north side of the town in 1888. That became known as North though the Caley tried to call it Town for a short period from 1906 onwards. However, it closed during the First World War from January 1917 to February 1919. The LMS renamed the ex-CR station North from 1924 but in July 1932, during the Depression and with an embarrassment of passenger facilities, they closed it for good. The final station with the prefix Ardrossan was another Caley facility named Montgomerie Pier – opened in 1890 on a spur from North station. It too suffered the same WWI fortunes as North station but after reopening in 1919 it was closed in the late 1930s, reopening again in June 1947 on a summer season only basis. It finally closed at the end of the summer timetable in September 1967. In this view the four platform layout provided by the optimistic Caley can still be seen. Tracks in the two dead-end platforms had been used for storage of late and the platforms themselves have been utilised for track component storage. The well-used tracks in the centre form the line to Montgomerie Pier, serving industrial premises en route. The refinery on the right appears to be a good source of income for BR.

A rather pleasing scene at Ardrossan (South Beach) station on Sunday afternoon, 17th May 1959. The train, headed by locally based 2P No.40667, was apparently headed for Largs having come from St Enoch. The passengers on the platform are awaiting the Ardrossan (Harbour) service. Note the attractive fares for Cheap Travel to Glasgow – 4/11d return and 3/- single. Note also the lack of canopies on the building gracing the Up platform.

Two years later, Stanier Cl.5 No.44992 crosses Holm junction and slows for the Ardrossan (South Beach) stop with a train from Largs to Kilmarnock on Monday 22nd May 1961. This aspect gives a clearer view of the four-road engine shed which was still doing business – and would for a number of years yet but not as an operational depot. The 4-6-0 was a new arrival at Hurlford engine shed having been transferred from St Rollox only days before to replace one of the growing throng of 2Ps which were being withdrawn. No.44992 itself would work until December 1966.

Ardrossan based 2F No.57266 hurries through South Beach station on 22nd May 1961 with a single brake van in tow. Its early morning shift completed, it was time for the 0-6-0 to retire to shed. Note that the Up side wooden buildings have been given a coat or two of paint whilst the poster now reveals that Cheap Travel to Glasgow is 5/6d return or 3/2d single. Considering inflation was pretty rampant in this period, the BR fares have not risen too much – or have they? – about 12%? The main passenger facilities at this station were to be found on the Down side platform.

The shearlegs on the west side of Ardrossan engine shed, 22nd May 1961, with a couple of prospective customers awaiting their turn. Typical of the steam age, at the depots of lesser importance, was the lack of shelter for the fitting staff. Of course, it was no better inside the shed where illumination usually consisted of an oil lamp. Hardy souls were those associated with the running and maintenance of the steam locomotive. However, one little gadget at Ardrossan did indicate that somebody cared at headquarters – the installation of a Lister diesel engine to power the hoist. A nice change from the chain driven, hand pulleys.

Having followed 2P No.40667 up to Largs on that Sunday afternoon of 17th May 1959, we see the 4-4-0 ready for departure at the head of the 4.00 p.m. to Glasgow. Note how clean the station platforms appear, a good advert for the day-trippers and holidaymakers who used BR for their journey to the coast. The station was opened in 1885 and is still doing business for the modern electric railway.

Making our way now from Largs to Kilmarnock, we reach Bogside Racecourse station on Monday 22nd May 1961 as Fowler 'Crab' No.42911 runs through with a short train of seven gunpowder vans. The locally based Mogul was on a duty which many railwaymen probably did not relish. Note the lack of a barrier wagon which would have been useless anyway if this lot had gone up. However, the carriage of gunpowder and other dangerous materials appears to have been relatively successful on Britain's railways over the years, with few if any incidents of note.

Shortly before the passage of the gunpowder train through Bogside Racecourse station on 22nd May 1961, a Down passenger train from St Enoch to Largs came through with Corkerhill 'Jubilee' No.45727 INFLEXIBLE in charge. The station here was also opened in 1885 but it was operated in conjunction with race days at the adjacent course and was known simply as Bogside. The suffix Racecourse was added by BR in 1952 but it reverted to Bogside in 1965. Besides catering for racegoers, the station had apparently, at some time in its history, handled trains carrying golfers, or spectators, for the nearby links; the latter was the more likely clientele as the thought of 300 or more golfers queuing to tee-off conjures up all sorts of difficulties! Closure of the station took affect from 2nd January 1967. The aforementioned 'Crab' can be seen in the background awaiting entry to the Down side sidings.

Turning inland on that same Monday in May 1961, we are on the route to Kilmarnock where Hurlford based (actually on loan from Corkerhill) BR Standard Cl.4 2-6-4T No.80000 is seen near Dreghorn with a Kilmarnock-Ardrossan passenger working.

Pulling away from Springside on 22nd May 1961, BR Standard Class 3 No.77018 has charge of the 9.04 a.m. Ardrossan-Kilmarnock 'stopper'. This former G&SW station opened in June 1890 and closed on 6th April 1964. Judging by the numbers of passengers leaving the station, the place must have been on Beeching's list. Five of the twenty-strong class of 2-6-0s, No.77015 to 77019, were allocated new to Hurlford in the summer of 1954 and all remained loyal to that shed except No.77019 which had eight months at Polmadie in 1963 to help with a motive power shortage at 66A; the Cl.3 did return to Hurlford though and was withdrawn from there with the other four during 1966. For some unexplained reason Polmadie's No.77007 was sent to Hurlford in August 1963 and also ended its days at 67B in 1966; perhaps the return of the Clayton diesels from remedial repairs gave 66A the incentive to rid themselves of their one and only BR Standard Cl.3.

With a porter waiting on the platform to hand over a crate to the guard, ex LMS 2P No.40638 draws into Crosshouse station on 22nd May 1961 with a Largs to Kilmarnock train. This station was sited at the junction of the lines from Ardrossan and the coastal stations to Kilmarnock, and the line to Glasgow via Dalry and Paisley from Kilmarnock. The latter route served the straight platforms, with the goods yard on the north side of the line. Although built some twenty-three years later than its predecessor, Crosshouse replaced an earlier station named Busby and was opened in April 1873. Note the lack of name boards and enamel signs proclaiming to passengers just where they were. However, the staff obviously had some pride in their station which is neat, clean and tidy – a strength which BR never tapped or indeed encouraged from their personnel in most places. This view was captured from the footbridge connecting the platforms. Closure at Crosshouse took affect from Monday 18th April 1966 for both sides of the station.

Situated just a few yards east of the passenger station, this is Crosshouse junction. On 22nd May 1961 a coast bound goods train is taking the line to Ardrossan under the watchful eye of the signal bobby.

Four days later a 'stranger in these parts' works through Crosshouse junction on Friday 26th May 1961. Gresley V3 No.67616 was in fact no stranger to these parts having been transferred to Hurlford from Parkhead in November 1960. Besides this particular 2-6-2T, Nos.67613, 67615, 67623, 67648, 67661, 67676 and 67679 arrived at Hurlford at the end of 1961, followed by 67607 and 67667 in February and March 1962 respectively; their job was to take the place of the ex LMS 2P 4-4-0s. V3 No.67613 had actually done time working from Ardrossan shed in 1960 and 1961 as the authorities tried desperately to find suitable work for the recently converted tank engines. No.67681 had transferred to Hurlford in November 1960 from Parkhead but was called back in February 1961 only to transfer again to 67B during the following October. Withdrawal took place just six weeks later. None of the other Gresley engines fared too well either as most were condemned at Hurlford shed by the early months of 1962. This V3 is far from being tested with the very lightly loaded 4.09 p.m. Kilmarnock to Ardrossan stopping train and must have thought (if such a thing was possible) that it had been 'put out to grass'. Basically it had. This illustration affords a better view of the diverging routes behind the train.

Another of the routes linking Kilmarnock with Glasgow was that through Lugton and Barrhead. On 22nd May 1961 one of Ayr's ex LMS 4F 0-6-0s No.44329 nears Kilmaurs with a northbound freight whilst a St Enoch-Kilmarnock passenger service steams away into the distance. 25

Ayr based 2P No.40610 looks rather resplendent at Kilmarnock on 29th June 1957 as it waits for departure with the 4.00 p.m. to Ayr. Alongside is Hurlford 2P No.40612 with the 3.38 p.m. working to Ardrossan. The cleanliness of the Ayr 4-4-0 has nothing to do with enthusiastic cleaners at 67C and more to do with the fact that No.40610 was recently ex works.

It is still not time for the two 2Ps to go their separate ways from Kilmarnock on that June afternoon in 1957 but whilst they are simmering at their respective bay platforms, the 10.35 a.m. Leeds (City)-Glasgow (St Enoch) has arrived behind 'Royal Scot' No.46108 SEAFORTH HIGHLANDER. We view the rather grubby 7P as it departs with the express – next stop Glasgow – which will travel via Crosshouse and Dalry. The ultimate express of the afternoon at Kilmarnock was the Down train of *THE THAMES-CLYDE EXPRESS* which would not yet have reached Carlisle. That named train departed St Pancras around 10.15 a.m. and after a long eight hours and fifty minutes journey would arrive St Enoch at about 7.00 p.m. Although having been running since September 1927, the train during the BR era was actually slower than the early LMS express. However, this Leeds-Glasgow working was far from dawdling on this date and had covered the 58 miles from the Dumfries stop in sixty minutes start to stop! Oh yes, and that was with a 445 ton load – standing room only!

27

Hurlford 2P No.40643 has just arrived from shed ready to take out a westbound passenger train from Kilmarnock on Sunday 17th May 1959. Note the height of the coal in the tender and the position of the fire irons, which are discernible to the left of the steam. This station opened in 1843 with alterations and enlargements carried out at various periods. Happily it is still open with four platforms operating but with only three of the four through roads illustrated here.

Another smart looking 2P at Kilmarnock but this is a Hurlford engine and the date is again 17th May 1959. No.40688 runs into the station with a service from Ardrossan. In the left background, in the fork of the Ayr and Ardrossan lines, is the former G&SWR locomotive works with its associated shops. Latterly Kilmarnock was used for storing and then scrapping mainly Scottish Region based locomotives although some former LMR locomotives were brought here for dismantling. Scrapping activity ceased at Kilmarnock on 4th July 1959 shortly after a large number of former LNER locomotives had been 'processed' in there. The engine illustrated was condemned in the same month that Kilmarnock closed and had to be taken all the way to Inverurie for cutting up.

Representing the goods engines working around Kilmarnock on that Sunday in May 1959 was ex Caley 0-6-0 No.57570 seen passing through the station. This engine had a long association with Hurlford shed having been allocated since early LMS days; it was at 67B where No.57570 was condemned in September 1961 but scrapping took place at Cowlairs. Note the home of a somewhat famous Scottish export forming a background to the 3F.

Kilmarnock locomotive works October 1953. The last survivor of the Caledonian 4P Pacific tanks, No.55359, awaits the inevitable. On the eve of Nationalisation there were nine of these large tank engines allocated to Beattock engine shed and employed exclusively on banking duties. Another, No.55355, was based at Greenock Ladyburn, the last of four which had been there on and off since at least the mid-1930s. Polmadie shedded the bulk of the class with eight of the original dozen allocated in the summer of 1935. However, during the latter years of World War II all twelve of these rather handsome engines were at Polmadie. So, what did Beattock manage with until the arrival of the 4-6-2T?; the answer, in April 1944 at least, was eleven ex Caley 0-4-4T. During the late summer of 1953 the compiler of this album was lucky enough to have had the pleasure of being on a northbound express which was pushed up Beattock bank by none other than our subject here – 55359. In those days, with drop-down windows and a certain amount of care, you could observe from the rear carriage all the effort expended by the last of these ninety-one ton Pacific tanks. They were getting a bit long in the tooth by Nationalisation and had passed their best. Of the final four in 1952, BR saw fit to condemn three of them by Easter whereas No.55359 hung on for another eighteen months! With no romantic notions as to what they were doing, the scrapmen at Kilmarnock cut up the 4-6-2 in January 1954.

Some old friends stable in Hurlford shed on 17th May 1959.

The scene presented on the west side of Hurlford shed on Sunday 21st May 1961. This area, behind the coal stage, was once the depot's coal stacking ground with a fan of sidings enabling equal distribution of the locomotive fuel. Now, only one siding is left and it is crowded with nine 2P 4-4-0s which were either stored or withdrawn. Inspection of the tenders at close quarters would reveal the BR crest, and the old emblems, the latter in two sizes, full lining, half lining and no lining. From right to left, the only engines identifiable are Nos.40626, 40592, and 40645. Hurlford always had a large complement of these 4-4-0s from early LMS days as they replaced the old G&SWR 4-4-0s. By September 1935 when the rout of the 'Sou West' engines was nearly complete, Hurlford had the following LMS 2Ps on its books: 570, 571, 572, 573, 574, 575, 590, 592, 597, 612, 618, 643, 644, 661, 662, 663, 664, 665, 686, 687, 688, and 689. Of course at this time Hurlford shed was still responsible for moving a fair proportion of the vast amounts of coal still being mined in Ayrshire and for that traffic twenty-four 0-6-0s of both LMS and Caley design were allocated. Wartime traffic patterns and demands brought changes to the types of motive power, and by the spring of 1944 the 2P complement was down to twenty engines whilst the 0-6-0 numbers had risen to thirty-two. When the end came for the 2P class in 1961, Hurlford could still muster a goodly number of them for the scrapman – note that none of this class were preserved. The shed itself was closed in October 1966.

With steam to spare Ayr based 2P No.40638 is seen near Darvel on 22nd May 1961. A later transfer to Stranraer would see the 4-4-0 condemned in June 1962.

As often happens, the rain arrives just after you have started your journey but on Sunday 17th May 1959 the journey of this photographer was by now nearly over having covered many of the railway routes around this south-western area of Scotland. Virtually following 2P No.40688 from Kilmarnock after its earlier arrival from Ardrossan, he has arrived at Darvel in time to see the 4-4-0 at the head of the 7.15 p.m. return to Kilmarnock. This Crewe-built 2P worked these routes for the whole of its life. Darvel was located some miles east of Kilmarnock on the Irvine valley line to Strathaven. Opened by the G&SWR in 1896, the station, serving a population of nearly 4,000 souls, was still nearly five years away from closure on this damp Sunday evening. Before closure, the passengers using this line were served by 4-wheel railbuses which ran right through to Ardrossan (Town).

(opposite) The fireman has just thrown on a round of coal prior to departure as Fowler 2-6-2T No.40049 stands at Muirkirk station with a stopping service to Kilmarnock on Monday 18th May 1959. This tank engine really was a 'stranger in town' – a one-off allocation to Hurlford from January 1959, courtesy of Willesden shed although it had been to Dundee Tay Bridge depot prior to its transfer to 67B. Willesden, or rather BR, were trying to find further employment for these Fowler tanks at this time and in desperation this engine was sent to Scotland. To give credit where it was due, the former LNER men at Dundee gave it a go and so did the LMS footplatemen on the Sou'-West but, they were having nothing to do with a rather disappointing locomotive type which nobody else wanted. It was returned to 1A in August 1959. Almost immediately Hurlford had another new type of 2-6-2T thrown at them in the shape of Stanier's version of the 3P, No.40151 from Dumfries – 67B kept hold of No.40151 until December 1962, when it was condemned. The coaching stock has been identified as a Period 1, Diagram 1746 BSO behind the locomotive. Built in 1926 at both Leeds Forge and LMS workshops, these vehicles were known as 'All Steels' with their design being integral and having no conventional underframe; the last of them worked up to 1962. The other two coaches are a SK and a BSK from Period 2 and built to a later, Stanier, design.

Two filthy ex Polmadie 4Fs, Nos.44322 and 44283, along with a much smarter Ardrossan 3F No.57566 enhance the shed yard at Muirkirk on Friday 30th August 1963 during an enthusiasts' visit. The shed here was originally a four-road structure dating from 1879 and built by the G&SW to house their own engines and a handful of Caley engines which worked to this coal-mining area from Carstairs. That arrangement continued through to Grouping and into the BR period as witnessed here. Hurlford supplied the motive power to Muirkirk, 2F and 3F 0-6-0s with a couple of 4-4-0s for the passenger services being the norm, although none are present on this occasion. With age and dilapidation catching up on it, not to mention a fire, the shed was reduced to two roads in the mid-50s' and this is how the place appeared at closure in October 1964.

A three-coach non-corridor consist gets the attention of a wheeltapper after arrival at Dumfries from Stranraer behind 2P No.40616 on 29th June 1957. In the Down platform a northbound parcels train pulls away with unknown motive power hauling an interesting mixture of stock. This particular station was the second to serve Dumfries and opened in 1859, with later extensions and additions. The finials on the platform canopy ridges are particularly worthy of inspection.

An all stations, evening service to Kilmarnock departs from Dumfries in the summer of 1959 behind Hurlford 2P No.40643. The train consist has a tidy combination of three Period 3, gangwayed, side-corridor Stanier coaches – BSK (Dia.1968)+SK (Dia.1899 or 2119)+BSK (Dia.1968), built between 1933 and 1950, and now in BR maroon livery – bringing up the rear, with an LMS Period 2 (Dia.1784), non-gangwayed All second behind the tender. The leading coach is in BR's earlier un-lined crimson livery and was one of 200 built at Derby between 1930 and 1933, with a further 78 erected at Wolverton in 1930.

Adding to the overcast, Kingmoor 'Crab' No.42913 works a freight bound for Stranraer through Dumfries station on Saturday 29th June 1957.

Carstairs allocated Class 5 No.45011 chooses the long route home as it leaves Dumfries behind whilst working a northbound freight on the morning of Saturday 29th June 1957. It is amazing to look back and realise how much freight traffic was on the move on British Railways on a Saturday during those far-off days of the 50s'. This engine spent the whole of its thirty year life working in Scotland firstly at Inverness and Perth and later at Eastfield, Hurlford, Grangemouth, Corkerhill and finally Carstairs from where it was withdrawn in December 1965. During the first three months of 1952 it was allocated to Kingmoor which although in England could be counted as Scottish territory simply because it was Caledonian in origin!

In the summer of 1952 'Royal Scot' No.46108 SEAFORTH HIGHLANDER departs Dumfries with *THE THAMES-CLYDE EXPRESS* – destination Glasgow (St Enoch). A resident of Leeds Holbeck shed since September 1943, this 'Scot' was one of the first in the class to benefit from the fitting of the 2A taper boiler and double chimney in August 1943. Having already clocked-up a mileage just short of one and a half million when this scene was captured on film, the 'Scot' was ready to add another half million to the total before being condemned in January 1963. According to records, its best year in traffic, mileage-wise, was 1957 when it managed nearly 75,000, working trains such as this. However, in that same year it had two months out of traffic undergoing a Heavy General overhaul at Crewe. Its return to Holbeck shed in mid-April 1957 must have seen it in fine fettle because it was from then onwards when most of those 70-odd thousand miles were run – more than 2,100 miles a week! In December 1958 it transferred to Longsight and was to spend the rest of its life working from Western Lines depots including Preston, Crewe North and finally, Upperby. On the right, and now undertaking a less hectic participation in express workings, an unidentified ex LMS 4P Compound sorts out some stock prior to working an evening departure to Stranraer. At this time Dumfries and Stranraer sheds had about a dozen of these 4-4-0s allocated between them.

(opposite) Another northbound working of *THE THAMES-CLYDE EXPRESS* approaches the Dumfries stop but this one is on Saturday 16th April 1960. The motive power is, as usual, a Holbeck 'Royal Scot' in the shape of No.46117 WELSH GUARDSMAN which, compared with No.46108 in the previous illustration, is looking somewhat grubby – a sign of the times? This of course is in the period just before the newly acquired, and Holbeck based, Gresley A3s took over the *TTCE* working prior to dieselisation.

Just south of the station at Dumfries, on the Up side of the line, was the engine shed. On a fine evening during the summer of 1958 when this view was captured from the Annan road bridge, the shed presented a fairly quiet yard to the group of visiting enthusiasts and the camera. A couple of 'Crabs' Nos.42908 and 42915, along with three ex Caley 0-6-0s numbered 57623, 57362, and 57302, and a solitary Class 5 No.45169 – all allocated to Dumfries – was all that could be mustered, although a similar number of locomotives were housed inside. All were coaled up, turned and ready for their next duties.

(*opposite*) One year later, during the morning of Sunday 14th June 1959, Dumfries shed yard was a little more crowded but most of the throng appear camera shy except a solitary Class 5, No.44670.

(opposite) Some thoughtful soul had vandalised the rear wall of the engine shed at Dumfries by apparently removing a number of bricks at the level where St Mary's Street crosses the main line. This desperate act, committed in order to view the inmates, enabled a generation of enthusiasts to photograph the resident engines when the right light conditions prevailed. The date is still Sunday 14th June 1959, with not a soul to be seen inside the building.

This undated view of the east side of Dumfries engine shed shows a few more of the resident 0-6-0s stabling in the area where firebox related stores were kept – firebricks for the arches, and timber for lighting the fires.

One of Corkerhill's BR Std. Cl.5s, No.73079, runs south of Dumfries with a short but interesting Up freight on 29th June 1957. The five wagons immediately behind the tender were new 12-ton ventilated vans built to Diagram 1/214. Vacuum braked, they were equipped with screw-link couplings and (strangely, for the period) spoked wheels. Only 100 were constructed, all at Wolverton in 1957. They were built for the specific transport of empty cans from Metal Box Co., at Carlisle to Libby's Creamery, at Milnthorpe near Carnforth. The vans had end loading doors at one end only, but a standard corrugated end at the other, with a ventilator hood. There were *no* side doors. In addition, LMS style, they had four torpedo vents on the roof which apparently was the only BR stock to be so fitted. Now it might have been brought to your attention that these vans were north of their intended 'corridor of work' which begs the question why? This compiler can only come up with the idea that the vans were facing the wrong way on delivery from Wolverton to Carlisle and were sent around the Sou'-West to turn them – its only an idea and stranger things have happened.

This is as far south as we travel – Annan. Another deserted station platform greets one of Kingmoor's Stanier Cl.5s, No.45118, as it heads towards Dumfries with a Glasgow bound express (it appears to be 1S44) on the last day of July 1965. The station here, which is still open today, was opened in August 1848. Another station in the town, but not on the main line, was that owned and opened by the Caley in 1869. It was called Shawhill from 1924 until closure in April 1931. At various periods in the past *THE THAMES-CLYDE EXPRESS* stopped at Annan. 49

Back to Dumfries on a rather damp day in May 1963, we find Cl.5 No.44967 standing at the head of a train bound for Kirkcudbright. Opened as long ago as February 1864, the ten-mile branch to Kirkcudbright veered south from the Stranraer road at Castle Douglas and, up to 1955, had its own engine shed. At least until the Second World War the tiny station could boast an overall roof, certainly at the terminal end. The 4-6-0 was too big for the turntable at Kirkcudbright, even if it was still available, so would have to work back to Dumfries tender first. The branch line closed on Monday 3rd May 1965, actually outliving this Cl.5 by nearly a year, the last train having worked off the branch on the previous Saturday headed by BR Standard Cl.4 No.76073. A month following that event, the whole route from Dumfries to Stranraer was closed and a large slice of Scottish railway history was completed. No.42196, the Cl.4 tank alongside, is another recent acquisition by Dumfries (the '5' had actually come in April) which had arrived from Hurlford in October 1962. Before 1963 was out, the tank would leave Scotland for Neville Hill, a depot which attracted many Class 4 tank engines from south-west Scotland. *D.H.Beecroft.*

Another northbound freight, albeit a short one, takes the Kilmarnock route out of Dumfries on Saturday 20th May 1961. Polmadie 'Clan' No.72004 CLAN MACDONALD is hardly being taxed during this its final full year of working. Considering it had only been out of Cowlairs works for a couple of months, after a Heavy General overhaul, No.72004 looks decidedly filthy, a state no doubt reflecting the contempt held at 66A for these engines. Records show that this particular Pacific, for one reason or another, consistently worked, per annum, very low or usually the least mileage within the class of ten. In 1961 for instance No.72004 ran just 22,394 miles, the lowest ever recorded for the class. During its best year some 49,559 miles were recorded but even that was low compared with many of the class which were showing annual mileage's in excess of 60,000 initially. Though much maligned, especially at the Scottish depots, the 'Clans' were somewhat under utilised or, as in this case, put onto the wrong workings. Ironically, in their last year of operation, No.72004 put up the highest mileage of all the 66A 'Clans' recording in excess of 35,000 miles. Withdrawn en masse on Saturday 29th December 1962, the five Polmadie 'Clans' 72000 to 72004, were eventually despatched to Darlington works for scrapping.

Kirkcudbright terminus, Tuesday 11th June 1957, with Stanier Cl.3 No.40151 at the head of an evening service to Dumfries. By now the overall roof of the station platform has been replaced with a simple canopy but the station itself was good for another eight years worth of traffic. It would be interesting and no doubt fascinating to read statistics such as traffic receipts, numbers of passengers handled, packages, goods, etc., for small termini like this. The ten mile long branch from the junction at Castle Douglas had three intermediate stations along its course: Castle Douglas (St Andrews Road) was only in fact a temporary station dating from the opening of the branch but necessary because the Board-of-Trade refused the use of the junction from branch to main line until August when a safer connection was completed. The station then passed into history except, according to some reports, for a brief period of opening in 1867. The next 'proper' station was Bridge of Dee which opened in April 1864 but closed in September 1949. Finally was Tarff which, like Kirkcudbright was operational throughout the life of the branch. The aforementioned engine shed was out of frame to the left.

On the Stranraer route now with a nicely turned-out Class 5, No.45480, setting off from Glenluce with a passenger working which includes a six-wheel milk tank in the formation on Saturday 24th May 1958. Glenluce, population 806, was 396 miles from London and the most westerly station on the line, or 'Port road' from Dumfries prior to the junction from Ayr joining the Stranraer line from the north. *David Dalton.*

Two views of the engine sheds at Stranraer on 28th March 1964 with, it will be noted, all the steam locomotives turned ready to work east out of town to either Dumfries or Glasgow and points in between. Stanier Class 5s predominate the scene with a BR Standard Cl.2 fitted up for light snow clearance work. One of the two Hunslet 0-6-0 diesel mechanical shunters allocated to Stranraer in 1958 is the only representation of the modern motive power. The Dumfries line remained a steam only route to closure and that is perhaps reflected in this scene. On the right is the branch leading down to the harbour, that particular route being the only surviving stretch of Stranraer's former railway system in 2011.

We are now at Stranraer (Town) station on Saturday 28th March 1964. BR Standard 2-6-4T No.80076 patiently waits in the bay platform with the 3-50 p.m. departure to Dumfries. Across the platform is one of the Swindon-built three-car diesel multiple units employed on services to Glasgow. The 4MT tank was a relative newcomer to Dumfries and its picturesque routes having been transferred from Ardsley during the previous October. Starting life on the London, Tilbury & Southend line in December 1953, the Standard had been progressively ousted out of work by electrification, dicsclisation and shortly by total lack of work because at the end of the forthcoming July it was condemned and then sold for scrap.

Heading north now, on the main line towards Ayr, we come across a couple of places which are no longer with us. The first is Pinmore, situated just south of Girvan and one of the few tunnels on the route – Pinmore tunnel. This is the deserted but still operational station on Sunday 17th April 1960. The lofty signal box was so typical of G&SW practice, and must have been a draughty and noisy place amidst this wind swept landscape. Pinmore station was opened in October 1877, closed on 7th February 1882 only to re-open nine days later on 16th February. In 1886 a similar event occurred when on 12th April it was closed with re-opening taking place on 14th June. For the next seventy-nine years it managed to keep its doors open until 6th September 1965. Not knowing the circumstances behind the two short closures it is difficult to speculate on what might have been. Weather could easily have been responsible for the first episode but the second and longer closure could not be easily explained away by snowdrifts in June. However, having experienced a blizzard in Scotland in July, admittedly on a ridge in the Highlands, this compiler is open to further suggestions and the real facts. Hopefully the station had a waiting room because externally the place is bereft of any awning, canopy or shelter.

Deviating from the main line just to the north of Girvan, we follow the 1906 coast line through Turnberry to Heads of Ayr, both places having totally different but nevertheless special meaning to many people. With the holiday camp in the right background, Stanier Cl.5 No.44724 departs from Heads of Ayr station with the 8.00 a.m. Saturdays Only to Newcastle – 1N08 – in August 1965. This Class 5 had been transferred to Ayr during the previous month from Perth and had not acquired any AWS apparatus. Although looking decidedly filthy, the 4-6-0 was operational for another fourteen months. The station here dated from July 1932 and replaced a 1906 vintage G&SWR station which closed in 1930. The LMS station was operating for the summer only and was then closed until May 1947 when it was re-opened to serve the adjacent Butlins establishment. Many thousands of people have used this station during the subsequent twenty-one years it operated, most, if not all of them, having a happy time from arrival to departure. Open for the duration of the summer seasons, and then on Saturdays only, the station handled its last train on Saturday 14th September 1968. *D.H.Beecroft.*

Before we reach Ayr, a little deviation to the south-east brings us to Dalmellington where, on Saturday afternoon 16th May 1959 ex LMS 2P No.40670 was working the branch passenger service. This branch opened in August 1856 to serve the coal and iron industries located in the area and today still exists to further serve the coal industry on what is now known as the Waterside branch. Dalmellington terminus and the branch passenger service closed in May 1964 whilst the branch line, kept open for coal traffic, was truncated at the next station – Waterside. Long before the closure to passengers the branch was worked by a Park Royal railbus. A disused engine shed at Dalmellington (through the trees not too far behind the engine), closed by the LMS in the early 30s', had a turntable which was in use until BR times but latterly it was beyond repair and the 4-4-0 had to work back to Ayr tender first. Shortly after this summer was over, No.40670 moved to Dumfries for a short period but then transferred to Ardrossan before finally settling at Dumfries where it became the last working example of its class. Withdrawal took place in December 1962, long before this end of the branch succumbed.

With a service from Kilmarnock, 2P No.40595 arrives at Ayr on a glorious Sunday morning, 17th May 1959. The coaching formation consists the following: Stanier, non-gangwayed, articulated, inter-district, 3-car set. Such sets were rare indeed as only eleven were ever built, and these were to Dia.1995 at Derby in 1937 (Lot 1038). Most were employed in Scotland and were withdrawn during 1963 and 1964. Note the number of compartment ventilators missing! The final vehicle is a pre-Grouping, passenger full brake which may well have been to a G&SWR design. The signals opposite the rear of the train appear to be an unusual configuration.

The grand and imposing station building at Ayr, incorporating the Station Hotel, is shown to effect on Sunday morning 17th May 1959. A service from Glasgow to Girvan has just arrived on the nearest platform whilst a departure for St Enoch, also from Girvan, stands at the opposite platform with a smart looking Fairburn 4P, Ayr's No.42194, at its head. Ayr shed had a number of these versatile and reliable tank engines allocated throughout the 50s'; others included 42122, 42131, 42195, 42196, 42197, 42201, and 42202. Once the summer timetable was completed this particular 2-6-4T would move on to Ardrossan.

Besides its seaside qualities, Ayr was also at the centre of the Ayrshire coalfield, an area still producing coal from a few opencast pits to this day. On 26th May 1961, 'Crab' No.42917, another 67C engine, has charge of a rather short, northbound, mineral working through Ayr station in glorious sunshine. In the first bay platform a DMU has just arrived from Glasgow whilst in the adjacent road a steam locomotive blows-off to add to the clamour of the station. Six-car DMUs were introduced onto the Glasgow-Ayr route in 1959 and gradually ousted the steam power.

One of the LMS-built Caley 2P 0-4-4Ts, No.55262, shunts an interesting mixture of stock into Townhead sidings at the south end of Ayr station, on Saturday 16th May 1959. Besides the rolling stock, look at the group of 'grounded' vehicles, in use as mess rooms, stores and workshops, on the platform. No.55262 spent much of its early life at Ayr but during WW2 it was transferred to Beattock where it joined ten other 0-4-4Ts on banking duties. It was condemned in September 1961, having returned to Ayr. For those of you interested in the wheeled vehicles they consisted: ex-LMS 6-wheel CCT (probably Dia.1872), Wolverton 1934; ex-LMS 42ft CCT [also known as Luggage & Parcels] van (probably Dia.1870), Wolverton 1934-37; LMS designed CCT (Motor Car Van), a number of which were built post-war to Dia.2026 at Swindon 1951-56; ex-LMS 50ft Passenger Full Brake (BG); Ditto; BR Mk1 57ft Passenger Full Brake (BG); SR 4-wheel CCT; ex-LNER 12-ton ventilated van; ex-LMS Stanier (Period 3), gangwayed SK; ex-LMS Stanier (Period 3), non-gangwayed BS; ex-LMS Stanier (Period 3), non-gangwayed All second. The 'bodies' on the platform are somewhat difficult to identify so any information – on a postcard please!

Complete with the old semaphore route indicator, a resplendent Corkerhill BR Std. Cl.4, No.80127, waits to depart from platform 1 at Ayr with a Glasgow train on 17th May 1959. This view shows the full width of the station and the covered area in its entirety. The station itself dates from January 1886 and replaced two earlier establishments located to the north of the present station. Happily, Ayr station is still doing business albeit for the electrified railway nowadays. New to Corkerhill in November 1955, the Class 4 tank wasn't four years old at the time of this photograph but premature withdrawal in July 1964 (it's turn for a heavy overhaul had arrived but such expense for steam locomotive repairs had just been made prohibitive), followed by scrapping in October, made sure it would never reach its ninth birthday. During their short lives on the Sou'-West section of Scottish Region, the BR 2-6-4Ts put in a comparable performance, and mileage to the Fairburn 2-6-4Ts with which they shared the same traffic, over the same routes. It is now time for us to head back from whence we came.

We have only travelled a short distance before we come to Newton-on-Ayr where the main line runs past the engine shed coded 67C by BR. From the footbridge linking the shed with the outside world, we can observe a Stanier Cl.5, No.45161, keeping a tight rein on a loaded northbound coal train, as it runs past the water tank at the south end of the shed yard in August 1965. By now relegated to duties such as this, the end is not too far away for these reliable locomotives in Ayrshire. *D.H.Beecroft.*

Contrasting styles at the southern end of the Galloway designed engine shed at Ayr, 17th April 1963. An extension has been built over the three western roads of the original six roads – this exercise being repeated at the north end so that diesel multiple units could be housed undercover from their arrival at Ayr in 1959. The three-road section on the eastern side is looking its age but would survive into the 1970s, unlike the steam locomotives gracing its roads in this illustration. The Thompson B1 is a new addition to the allocation at 67C having been sent from Corkerhill, who initially got it for Christmas 1962 from Eastfield. Just eleven years old at this time, and the youngest engine in view, the 4-6-0 moved back to more familiar territory at St Margarets in July 1964.

Besides the working Class 5s in the Ayr district during August 1965, there was inevitably those that had reached the end – No.45460 was one of those. Withdrawn during the previous June, the 4-6-0 stands on one of the lonely and now redundant coal stack roads in the middle of the triangle surrounding Ayr shed. Built in 1938 and put into traffic at Perth in October of that year, the '5' was to spend exactly nineteen years working from that shed (a three week loan to Dundee in March 1950 doesn't count). Inverness was the next depot to use its power and it worked from there until May 1960 when it came south to Corkerhill to spend the rest of its life on the Sou-West'. It was transferred to Ayr in August 1962. No.45460 was sold for scrap to Arnott Young who took it into their yard at nearby Troon for cutting up. *D.H.Beecroft.*

Carrying target A43, Class 5 No.45474 blasts round the north to east side of the triangle at Ayr with mineral empties for Annbank in August 1965. The engine shed was to the left of the frame, where the smoke was heading. *D.H.Beecroft.*

With the time showing 9.20 a.m. on the station clock, one of the Corkerhill based BR Std. Cl.5s, No.73100, takes a brief rest at Barassie whilst working a morning service from St Enoch to Ayr on Monday 22nd May 1961. The line from Kilmarnock curves in from the right. Barassie was the site chosen by the G&SWR for their carriage and wagon works which became operational in 1901 on a 22 acre site nearby. In 1929 carriage repair was moved to Glasgow and Barassie then concentrated on wagon repair. During WW2, like many of the railway workshops in Britain, Barassie took on war work for the Government. Being on fairly flat terrain, whilst located on the west coast, the works was extended and then a runway built so that Spitfire aircraft could be overhauled. After the cessation of hostilities, wagon repairs continued at Barassie long into the BR period but the works closed in 1972. The carriage and wagon shops even had its own station for the workforce, aptly named Barassie Workshops. The junction station illustrated had its origins back in 1848 and once had the name Barassie Junction; it is still open today but the Kilmarnock route platforms are disused whilst the route itself has been singled and is for freight only. In an age when platform illumination was minimal to say the least, the platform edge painting provides a different aspect to passenger safety but why paint the vertical surface?

Polmadie based Caley 0-6-0 No.57581 provides the motive power with an enthusiasts special at Lanark Racecourse station on Saturday 20th October 1962. Departing from St Enoch terminus at 10.30 that day, the railtour was entitled 'The Covenanter' a somewhat unconventional* name. Besides this 'occasional station' being under inspection, the signal box has also become the focus of attention for many. Despite being geographically on the very edge of our survey area, this station deserves inclusion because of its status. Opened in August 1910, and used only for military and race traffic, the facility closed completely on 27th September 1964 but when the last race-goers actually used the station is unknown. The timber construction of the platform faces and edges appears to have stood up nicely to fifty-odd years of weather, whilst the platform surfaces are a mixture of gravel, ideal for occasional use! Note the two grounded but well-cared for rail vehicles on the opposite platform. It is nice to see that 66A bothered to brighten up their 0-6-0 with a lick of paint here and there alongside the application of paraffin rags. Finally, the only train identification is a chalked letter Z on the oblong plate affixed to the centre lamp-iron (a printed and pasted paper 1 was in situ at the start of the railtour); at that period Z usually meant special working which this obviously was.

* The original 'Covenanters' were Scots people, mostly Lowlanders, who signed the National Covenant in 1638. By so doing, they confirmed their opposition to the interference by the Stuart Kings in the affairs of their Presbyterian church. The Stuart Kings, of course, believed in the 'Divine right of the Monarch' – look what happened to Charles in London! I suppose the name of the railtour reflected the area it was visiting.

Paisley (Gilmour Street) station, Tuesday 20th April 1965. Cl.4 No.42694 (you will have to take my word for it) has charge of the 10.40 a.m. Glasgow (Central)-Wemyss Bay service. A sign of the times was the matelot travelling in uniform, a period when servicemen generated a certain amount of pride for 'the man in the street' and security of military personnel was not even considered because there were no such issues. Another sign of those times was the condition of the tank engine – filthy and unkempt! No.42694, as mentioned earlier, was now allocated to Greenock Ladyburn shed having transferred from Dawsholm during the previous July. The 2-6-4T had less than a month to work these passenger services because in May it was moved to Carstairs. We are working our way back to Glasgow and will catch the next train which will take us on the final leg. Our journey has been somewhat circuitous, with an element of doubling back at some locations but isn't that what we did anyway when we travelled by rail in those days.

What better place to finish our imaginary tour than the same terminus where we started – St Enoch. It is now early afternoon on a date to be determined but certainly after March 1960 (*see below*). It is sunny but clouds are building and perhaps threatening in the west. We are now on the west side of the station with a Kingmoor Cl.5 No.44672 standing at platform 12 with non-corridor stock. At platform 10 is BR Standard Class 4 tank No.80047 (one of the last steam locomotives to receive a major overhaul at any of the Scottish works, in April 1964), with similar stock. The tank engine was based at Corkerhill and transferred there from Chester in March 1960. Note that the South-Western lines route indicator, normally carried on the central lamp-iron above the bufferbeam, is absent which might give a further clue as to the date. As already mentioned in the opening caption on page 3, extensions were carried out and completed here in 1902 giving St Enoch six more platforms (7 to 12), again under a magnificent arched roof. Though not as big as the earlier covering, the new roof incorporated an arch of 143ft span, covering 294 linear feet of the new platforms and was 65ft high. As can be seen, awnings completed the platform coverage. It may be worth mentioning that the original intention of the G&SWR was to construct a through station here, on the same east-west heading, but the terminal idea won the day. It will be noted that semaphore signals are absent from St Enoch because colour-light signals were installed here by the LMS as early as 1932 to help speed up operations and ease the congestion suffered by the terminus at that time. Besides the numerous steam hauled passenger trains still using the station, St Enoch was playing host to a growing number of diesel multiple units and main-line locomotives on the Anglo-Scottish services during the early Sixties'. However, on Sunday 26th June 1966, all that was to change when the station entertained its last passengers, official closure taking place next day. Immediately behind the photographer, in the triangle created by the west-north-south-west junctions, there stood the one-time engine shed which shared the same name as the station but which outgrew its usefulness in 1932 and was thereafter used for seasonal storing of locomotives. This building too, despite being an engine shed, was quite magnificent and still in existence and in railway use when St Enoch closed. In 1977, after years of playing the role of a glorified car park, the terminal station was demolished along with the engine shed to the east of the site. They call it progress. A large glass-roofed shopping centre (still apparently expanding) occupies the site of St Enoch terminus now.